Exceptional African Americans

KOBE BRYANT

All-Star Shooting Guard

Joseph Kampff

Enslow Publishing
101 W. 23rd Street
Suite 240
New York, NY 10011
USA

enslow.com

Words to Know

assist—When a player passes the ball to a teammate who makes a basket.

clutch—The ability to make shots at important moments.

draft—The way NBA teams pick new players each year.

endorsement—A business deal in which a person is paid to say he or she likes a product.

freshman—A first-year student in high school or college.

NBA (National Basketball Association)—A group of professional basketball players.

professional—Paid to play a sport or activity.

recruiter—A person who tries to get athletes to go to a particular college.

varsity—The top team at a school.

Contents

Kobe Bryant

CHAPTER 1

Born to Play Ball

Who is the greatest player in the history of basketball? Many people would say Michael Jordan. But Kobe Bryant is also a strong choice for best player of all time. In fact, Kobe passed Jordan on the **NBA's** all-time scoring list in 2014.

Kobe was born on August 23, 1978, in Philadelphia, Pennsylvania. His father, Joe "Jellybean" Bryant is a former NBA player and basketball coach. Kobe's mother, Pam Bryant, is the sister of former NBA player Chubby Cox. It is no surprise that Kobe started

Kobe attends a baseball game with his father, Joe "Jellybean" Bryant, who was also a professional basketball player.

playing basketball when he was three years old. He was born with basketball in his blood.

Italian Lessons

When Kobe was six years old, his family moved to Italy so his father could continue playing **professional** basketball. Learning how to play basketball in Italy helped Kobe become the player he is today. Kobe says that kids' basketball in

Europe is different than in the United States. They focus more on practice and learning basics than on playing games.

The Bryant family moved back to the United States in 1991. When Kobe returned to his hometown, he could speak Italian. He also brought back the skills he'd learned on the court.

Kobe Says:

"When I started out on this journey, I was just infinitely curious about the game of basketball . . . I was just fascinated by it. You start understanding really early that everything around you is an opportunity to learn."

CHAPTER 2

Chasing the Dream

Kobe was always ahead of the game. As a **freshman**, he played on the **varsity** team at Lower Merion High School in Philadelphia. Most freshmen don't get to play on the varsity team. Kobe quickly showed that he was a star on the court.

In his third year of high school, Kobe had an average of 31.1 points, 10.4 rebounds, and 5.1 **assists** per game. Kobe led his team to a state championship in 1996. He even broke Wilt Chamberlain's record for most points scored in

Kobe dunks the ball in the gym at his high school in 1996.

Kobe returned to his old high school in 2002 when his jersey number was retired.

a high school career. **Recruiters** from the best college basketball programs had their eyes on him.

Kobe had a great high school career. But even then he was ahead of the game. During the summer, Kobe took his game to the gym at St. Joseph's University. A lot of players from the Philadelphia 76ers practiced there. Kobe had no problem playing with the pros.

Kobe Says:

"I felt real comfortable all summer with the guys. I had no butterflies, no nothing. [I] never felt intimidated. I could get to the hole. I could hit the jumper. After a while it kind of popped into my mind that I can play with these guys."

CHAPTER 3

Taking Chances

Kobe was the best high school basketball player in the country. He could have played ball at any college. But Kobe wanted to play in the NBA as soon as possible. He wanted to be as great as players like Michael Jordan and Magic Johnson. "I have decided to skip college and take my chances in the NBA," Kobe explained. "I know I'll have to work hard, and I know this is a big step, but I can do it."

Kobe was chosen in the first round of the 1996 NBA **draft** by the Charlotte Hornets. The Hornets traded

When Kobe was growing up, he admired NBA players like Michael Jordan (left).

Kobe to the Los Angeles Lakers two weeks later. The Lakers had been Kobe's favorite team since he was a kid. His dream had become a reality.

A Rocky Start

Kobe may have been an amazing player in high school, but playing in the NBA is much harder.

Kobe holds up his jersey after joining the Los Angeles Lakers in 1996. Standing with him are the team's general manager Jerry West (left) and head coach Del Harris.

At the time, Kobe was the youngest player to play in the NBA. It took him a while to get used to it. In fact, Kobe shot four airballs in the last few minutes of the Lakers playoff game against the Utah Jazz. The Lakers lost the game and were knocked out of the playoffs.

Even though it was a big loss, Kobe's teammates were not mad at him. Shaquille O'Neal explains, "I wasn't upset that he shot those airballs. He was the only one with enough guts to shoot the ball." Kobe kept working on his game and is now known as one of the most **clutch** shooters in basketball history.

Kobe Says:

"If you're afraid to fail, then you're probably going to fail."

Kobe has also kept busy off the court. He married dancer Vanessa Laine in 2001 and they have two daughters, Natalia and Gianna.

Kobe's family (left to right: Natalia, Gianna, and wife Vanessa) enjoy a Lakers game.

CHAPTER 4

The Greatest of All Time?

Kobe Bryant is one of the hardest-working players ever. He never stops working to improve his game. He studies the moves of other great players so he can play like them. Kobe's favorite player is Michael Jordan.

Kobe helped the Lakers to win three championships in a row in 2001, 2002, and 2003. With Kobe and Shaq playing at the top of their games, the Lakers were unstoppable. Their coach, Phil Jackson, was one of the best coaches in the NBA. He had already won six championships with the Chicago Bulls. Kobe's Lakers

Kobe Says:

"Everything negative—pressure, challenges—is all an opportunity for me to rise."

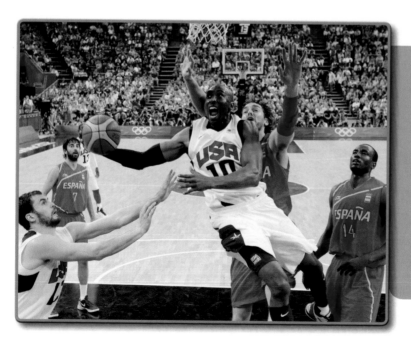

Kobe jumps for a basket during the gold medal game against Spain in the 2012 London Olympics.

won championships again in 2009 and 2010. Kobe also helped the US Olympics team win gold medals in 2008 and 2012.

At the Top of His Game

Success on the court has led to success in business. Kobe signed his first **endorsement** deal with the shoe company Adidas. The deal earned him 48 million dollars. Since then he has made deals with lots of companies, including Coca-Cola and McDonald's. He even started his own line of shoes with Nike. His job with the Lakers and his endorsement deals make Kobe one of the highest paid athletes in the world.

Not everybody likes Kobe. He's one of the most aggressive players ever to play basketball. He has been called a ball hog by people who think he takes too many shots. He has also made a lot of those shots. Only two other players have scored more

Kobe teaches basketball to children in China as part of a Nike program.

than him: Karl Malone and Kareem Abdul-Jabbar. And, in fact, Kobe has more assists in his career than Michael Jordan.

Kobe's goal in life is to be the greatest player in basketball. Has he succeeded? The question of who is the greatest player might be impossible to answer. But Kobe's greatness cannot be denied.

Kobe dunks the ball during a 2013 Lakers game against the Minnesota Timberwolves.

Timeline

1978—Kobe Bryant is born in Philadelphia, Pennsylvania.

1984—Moves to Italy with his family.

1992–1996—Plays varsity basketball at Lower Merion High School in Philadelphia.

1996—Selected by the Charlotte Hornets in the first round of the NBA draft. Traded to the Los Angeles Lakers.

2001–2003—Wins three NBA championships in a row with the Lakers.

2008—Wins Olympic Gold Medal in Beijing. Named NBA Most Valuable Player.

2009—Wins fourth NBA championship.

2010—Wins fifth NBA championship.

2012—Wins Olympic Gold Medal in London.

2014—Passes Michael Jordan's all-time scoring record.

Learn More

Books

The Editors of Sports Illustrated Kids. *Sports Illustrated Kids Slam Dunk! Top 10 Lists of Everything in Basketball.* New York: Time Home Entertainment, Inc., 2014.

Kelley, K.C. *2014 Basketball Superstars (NBA)*. New York: Scholastic, Inc., 2014.

Osier, Dan. *Kobe Bryant*. New York: PowerKids Press, 2011.

Websites

kobebryant.com
Official website with news and videos about Kobe Bryant.

nba.com/playerfile/kobe_bryant/
Player profile with biography, career statistics, and news.

Index

Published in 2016 by Enslow Publishing, LLC.
101 W. 23rd Street, Suite 240, New York, NY 10011

Copyright © 2016 by Enslow Publishing, LLC.
All rights reserved.

No part of this book may be reproduced by any means without the written permission of the publisher.

Library of Congress Cataloging-in-Publication Data
Kampff, Joseph.
    Kobe Bryant : all-star shooting guard / Joseph Kampff.
        pages cm. — (Exceptional African Americans)
    Includes bibliographical references and index.
    Summary: "Describes the life and career of Kobe Bryant"—Provided by publisher.
    ISBN 978-0-7660-7258-9 (library binding)
    ISBN 978-0-7660-7256-5 (pbk.)
    ISBN 978-0-7660-7257-2 (6-pack)
    1. Bryant, Kobe, 1978—Juvenile literature. 2. Basketball players—United States—Biography—Juvenile literature. I. Title.
    GV884.B794K36 2016
    796.323092—dc23
    [B]
                    2015030836

Printed in the United States of America

To Our Readers: We have done our best to make sure all website addresses in this book were active and appropriate when we went to press. However, the author and the publisher have no control over and assume no liability for the material available on those websites or on any websites they may link to. Any comments or suggestions can be sent by e-mail to customerservice@enslow.com.

Photo Credits: Throughout book, ©Toria/Shutterstock.com (blue background); cover, p. 1 Stacy Revere/Getty Images Sport/Getty Images; p. 4 Michael Kovac/WireImage/Getty Images; pp. 6, 9, 10, 16, 18, 21 © AP Images; p. 13 Sporting News Archive/Sporting News/Getty Images; p. 14 Steve Grayson/WireImage/Getty Images; p. 20 ChinaFotoPress/ChinaFotoPress/Getty Images.